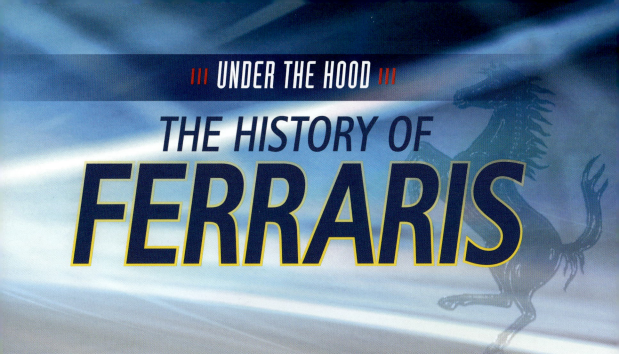

||| UNDER THE HOOD |||

THE HISTORY OF FERRARIS

SETH KINGSTON

NEW YORK

Published in 2019 by The Rosen Publishing Group, Inc.
29 East 21st Street, New York, NY 10010

Copyright © 2019 by The Rosen Publishing Group, Inc.

All rights reserved. No part of this book may be reproduced in any form without permission in writing from the publisher, except by a reviewer.

Copyright 2012; reprint 2019

Editor: Elizabeth Krajnik
Book Design: Michael Flynn

Photo Credits: Cover (car) VanderWolf Images/Shutterstock.com; cover, p. 1 (emblem) TOM.RUETHAI/Shutterstock.com; cover, pp. 1, 3–6, 8, 10, 12, 14–18, 20–26, 28, 30–32 (background) fotomak/Shutterstock.com; p. 5 (812 Superfast) Michael Dodge/Getty Images News/Getty Images; p. 5 (Portofino) Zavatskiy Aleksandr/Shutterstock.com; pp. 7 (815), 15 (Ferrari 340) Klemantaski Collection/Hulton Archive/Getty Images; p. 7 (125 S) LagunaticPhoto/Shutterstock.com; p. 9 (166 MM) Michael Cole/Corbis Sport/Getty Images; p. 9 (logo) Frank11/Shutterstock.com; p. 10 dimcars/Shutterstock.com; p. 11 Seung-il Ryu/NurPhoto/Getty Images; p. 13 Dan74/Shutterstock.com; p. 15 (main) Mr Zap/Shutterstock.com; p. 16 Grzegorz Czapski/Shutterstock.com; p. 17 Sergey Kohl/Shutterstock.com; p. 19 (top) oksana.perkins/Shutterstock.com; p. 19 (bottom) Mike FANOUS/Gamma-Rapho/Getty Images; p. 21 (bottom) Pavlo Baliukh/Shutterstock.com; p. 21 (top) Leena Robinson/Shutterstock.com; pp. 22–23 Alberto Zamorano/Shutterstock.com; p. 24 bepsy/Shutterstock.com; p. 25 AmorSt-Photographer/Shutterstock.com; p. 27 Jens Mommens/Shutterstock.com; p. 29 Jack Taylor/Getty Images News/Getty Images.

Cataloging-in-Publication Data

Names: Kingston, Seth.
Title: The history of Ferraris / Seth Kingston.
Description: New York : PowerKids Press, 2019. | Series: Under the hood | Includes glossary and index.
Identifiers: ISBN 9781538344521 (pbk.) | ISBN 9781538343388 (library bound) | ISBN 9781538344538 (6 pack)
Subjects: LCSH: Ferrari automobile–Juvenile literature. | Ferrari automobile–History–Juvenile literature.
Classification: LCC TL215.F47 K56 2019 | DDC 629.222–dc23

Manufactured in the United States of America

CPSIA Compliance Information: Batch #CWPK19: For Further Information contact Rosen Publishing, New York, New York at 1-800-237-9932

CONTENTS

THE FERRARI LEGACY 4
ITALIAN BEGINNINGS 6
EARLY FERRARIS 8
EVERYDAY FERRARIS 10
FERRARIS ON THE TRACK 12
FORMULA ONE CHAMPIONS 14
THE TESTAROSSA: 1984–1996 16
THE ENZO FERRARI: 2002–2004 18
THE CALIFORNIA: 2008–2017 20
THE 458 ITALIA: 2009–2015 22
THE FF: 2011–2016 24
THE SF71H 26
70 YEARS AND BEYOND 28
TIMELINE 30
GLOSSARY 31
INDEX 32
WEBSITES 32

THE FERRARI LEGACY

Since 1947, Ferrari has been producing world-class racecars and sports cars. They're some of the most desired, or wanted, cars in the world. Because Ferrari doesn't make very many of each car, many people have to sign up on a waiting list. Ferraris are also some of the most expensive cars in the world.

The Ferrari **legacy** began with just one man—Enzo Ferrari—and one car—the 125 S. This car laid the company's base in sports car manufacturing and racing. Today, Ferrari is famous for its sports cars with 12-**cylinder**, or V-12, engines. Most **passenger** cars have engines with four or six cylinders. These extra cylinders make drivers feel like they're speeding around a racetrack when they're really just driving down regular roads!

> FERRARI SELLS A RANGE OF PASSENGER CARS. SOME HAVE V-12 ENGINES, SUCH AS THE 812 SUPERFAST, WHILE OTHERS, SUCH AS THE PORTOFINO, HAVE V-8 ENGINES.

PORTOFINO

812 superfast

ITALIAN BEGINNINGS

On February 18, 1898, Enzo Anselmo Ferrari—the founder of Ferrari—was born in Modena, Italy. When Ferrari was just 10 years old, he decided he wanted to be a racecar driver. His dream came true in 1919, when he and fellow driver Ugo Sivocci competed in a race called the Targa Florio. The next year, Ferrari and Sivocci drove for Alfa Romeo, an Italian car manufacturer, in the Targa Florio.

In 1939, Ferrari left Alfa Romeo to create his own car manufacturing company, Auto Avio Costruzioni. Ferrari's new company's first car, produced in 1940, was an open-topped, eight-cylinder sports car called the 815. In late 1943, Ferrari moved Auto Avio Costruzioni's workshops from Modena to Maranello, Italy. There, Ferrari built the first car bearing his name—the 125 S.

ONLY TWO 815s WERE MADE AND THEY WERE NEVER CALLED FERRARIS. THE 815, PICTURED HERE, WAS BUILT IN JUST FOUR MONTHS AND PARTICIPATED IN THE 1940 MILLE MIGLIA.

THE FIRST FERRARI

The 125 S was a 12-cylinder sports car meant for racing. Ferrari took the 125 S on its first road test on March 12, 1947, and it made its racing debut, or first official appearance, at the Piacenza circuit on May 11, 1947. The 125 S won its first race in the Rome Grand Prix at the Terme di Caracalla circuit on May 25, 1947.

EARLY FERRARIS

In 1948, Ferrari launched a number of different models. The 166 S, which was launched in early 1948, was a racecar that came as either a coupe, which is a hardtop car with two doors, or a spider, which is a convertible. Ferrari built a **prototype** based on the 166 S called the 166 Sport, but the name was soon changed to the 166 Inter.

The 166 MM, which was also based on the 166 S, was **designed** for **endurance** racing. The MM stands for the Mille Miglia, one of the world's most famous road races.

The 166 Inter was the road type of the 166 MM and was produced from 1948 to 1950. This model was a key player in Ferrari's success outside Italy and helped the company enter the American sports car market.

THE 166 MM IS VERY LIGHT AND **AERODYNAMIC**. HOWEVER, ITS FRAME IS FAIRLY STIFF TO PREVENT IT FROM BEING CRUSHED IN THE EVENT OF A CRASH.

THE BIRTH OF THE LOGO

The Ferrari logo is a black stallion prancing, or rearing up on its hind legs, on a yellow background. The story goes that, one day, while he was still racing for Alfa Romeo, Ferrari met the parents of Francesco Baracca, who was a World War I pilot. His plane had a prancing black stallion on it. Baracca's parents asked Ferrari to put this image on his cars as a **symbol** of good luck. Today, all Ferraris have the prancing black stallion logo.

EVERYDAY FERRARIS

Ferrari aims to stay true to its racing roots, and a number of things set Ferrari apart from its competitors. It produces fewer units of its models each year, its cars have Formula-One-style paddle shifters, and the cars' engines produce a one-of-a-kind sound.

Ferrari has never offered a two-seat sports car in all-wheel drive or four-wheel drive. However, the company has offered these choices in its four-seat sports cars. Ferrari has also never made a sport-utility vehicle (SUV). Because the company's history is so deeply rooted in racing, company leaders say, offering a SUV would take away from its aims.

TO MARK FERRARI'S 70TH ANNIVERSARY IN 2017, THE COMPANY DESIGNED THE LAFERRARI APERTA FOR THE BRAND'S MOST PASSIONATE CLIENTS. ONE CUSTOMER PURCHASED A NEW 2017 LAFERRARI APERTA FOR ALMOST $10 MILLION.

As of 2018, Ferrari produces nine models. The 812 Superfast and the GTC4Lusso have V-12 engines. The 812 Superfast is the fastest and most powerful Ferrari produced so far. The GTC4Lusso is a four-seat sports car with four-wheel drive.

FERRARIS ON THE TRACK

Ferrari has produced racecars since the company was founded. Each year, Ferrari produces new racecars that are lighter, faster, and safer than before. Ferrari's first racecar, the 125 S, raced in 14 races and won six. Today, Ferrari produces cars for Formula One (F1) racing, Grand Touring (GT) racing, and Corse Clienti (customer racing). However, Scuderia Ferrari, the company's racing team, only takes part in F1 racing.

In 1949, Ferrari won its first 24 Hours of Le Mans. In 1953, Ferrari won the first Sportscar World Championship title. Today, Ferrari produces four models for GT teams: the 488 GTE, the 488 GT3, the 458 Italia GTE, and the 458 Italia GT3. Ferrari has won 24 manufacturers' titles for GT, including the World Cup for Manufacturers of the World Endurance Championship in 2012, 2013, 2014, 2016, and 2017.

> AS OF 2018, THE 488 CHALLENGE IS THE CAR BEING RACED IN ALL CATEGORIES OF THE FERRARI CHALLENGE. IT'S THE MOST POWERFUL CAR IN FERRARI CHALLENGE HISTORY, WITH A 670-HORSEPOWER V-8 ENGINE.

CORSE CLIENTI

Ferrari Corse Clienti allows customers interested in racing their cars to take part in activities just for Ferrari owners. The Ferrari Challenge is a one-make series established in 1993. There are three separate championships in the Europe, North America, and Asia-Pacific regions. Each region has three categories, or classes, including Trofeo Pirelli, Trofeo Pirelli Am, and Coppa Shell. Corse Clienti is responsible for organizing the three championships of the Ferrari Challenge Trofeo Pirelli.

FORMULA ONE CHAMPIONS

In 1950, the Fédération Internationale de l'Automobile (FIA) created a new category of racing—Formula One. Scuderia Ferrari didn't take part in the first F1 race but competed in a Formula Two race at Mons in Belgium, where Ferraris took first, second, and third places. On May 21, 1950, Scuderia Ferrari made its F1 debut at the Monaco Grand Prix.

F1 cars are the fastest racecars in the world. They race at speeds of up to 220 miles (354.1 km) per hour. F1 teams compete in a series of races around the world called grands prix. Teams earn points based on how they finish, and whichever team has the most points at the end of the season wins. Scuderia Ferrari is the most successful team in F1 history.

SCUDERIA FERRARI'S MOST FAMOUS DRIVER IS MICHAEL SCHUMACHER, WHO DROVE FOR THE TEAM FROM 1996 TO 2006. DURING THAT TIME, SCHUMACHER COMPETED IN 180 GRANDS PRIX, OF WHICH HE WON 72. HE HAS SEVEN F1 WORLD CHAMPIONSHIP TITLES, FIVE OF THEM WITH FERRARI.

||| START YOUR ENGINES |||

SCUDERIA FERRARI HOLDS MANY RECORDS. IT HAS THE MOST CONSTRUCTOR CHAMPIONSHIPS, WITH 16. "CONSTRUCTOR" MEANS THAT THE TEAM MADE ITS OWN CAR. IT ALSO HOLDS THE RECORD FOR MOST DRIVER CHAMPIONSHIPS WITH 15.

FERRARI 340 F1

THE TESTAROSSA
1984–1996

One of Ferrari's most iconic cars is the Testarossa, which made its debut at the Paris Motor Show in October 1984. *Testarossa* means "redhead" in Italian and refers to the color of an engine part on the 1957 Ferrari 250 Testa Rossa sports racing car. The Testarossa was Ferrari's most expensive car at the time, but it was so popular that it outsold Ferrari's cheaper cars. The Testarossa was made from 1984 until 1996. Nearly 10,000 units were sold during that time.

> IN 1992, FERRARI LAUNCHED THE 512 TR AS A CHANGE TO THE TESTAROSSA AT THE LOS ANGELES AUTO SHOW. IN 1994, ANOTHER CHANGE TO THE TESTAROSSA CALLED THE F512M WAS LAUNCHED AT THE PARIS AUTO SHOW.

512 TR TESTAROSSA

||| START YOUR ENGINES |||

THE TESTAROSSA HAD A 380-HORSEPOWER, 12-CYLINDER ENGINE, AND A FIVE-SPEED MANUAL **TRANSMISSION.** IT COULD GO FROM 0 TO 60 MILES (0 TO 96.6 KM) PER HOUR IN 5.3 SECONDS AND REACH A TOP SPEED OF 175 MILES (281.6 KM) PER HOUR.

F512 M TESTAROSSA ENGINE

The Testarossa's design, created by Italian design company Pininfarina, broke away from the usual Ferrari look. It appeared more futuristic and striking than previous models. It was wider and had sharper lines than earlier Ferraris. Its most notable features were the long side strakes, or vents, which helped make the Testarossa more aerodynamic.

17

THE ENZO FERRARI 2002–2004

The Enzo Ferrari debuted at the 2002 Paris Motor Show. The Enzo was a very **exclusive** car. Only 399 units were produced and sold at first, but Ferrari built 50 more soon after. At the time the car was launched, each one cost more than $650,000.

The Enzo used F1 technology in a road car package. The car was very aerodynamic and was smaller and lighter than other Ferraris. The inside of the car was very simple. It had all the control buttons around the steering wheel, just like in a racecar.

The Enzo had a V-12 engine that produced 660 horsepower. It could go from 0 to 60 miles (0 to 96.6 km) per hour in just 3.5 seconds and reach speeds of up to 220 miles (354.1 km) per hour. The Enzo had butterfly doors, which open out and up rather than only opening out.

> THE ENZO WAS NAMED AFTER ENZO FERRARI, THE COMPANY'S FOUNDER, WHO DIED ON AUGUST 14, 1988. ONE OF THE ENZOS WAS PAINTED *ROSSO DINO*, OR "DINO RED" IN ITALIAN, TO HONOR ENZO FERRARI'S SON DINO, WHO DIED AS A YOUNG MAN.

FOR A GOOD CAUSE

In January 2005, Ferrari gifted the 400th Enzo Ferrari to Pope John Paul II. The pope asked Ferrari to sell the car for him and give the money to the people affected by the **tsunami** that hit Southeast Asia in 2004. The car was sold in June 2005 for $1.1 million and the money was presented to the next pope, Pope Benedict XVI. In 2015, the car was sold again for $6,050,000.

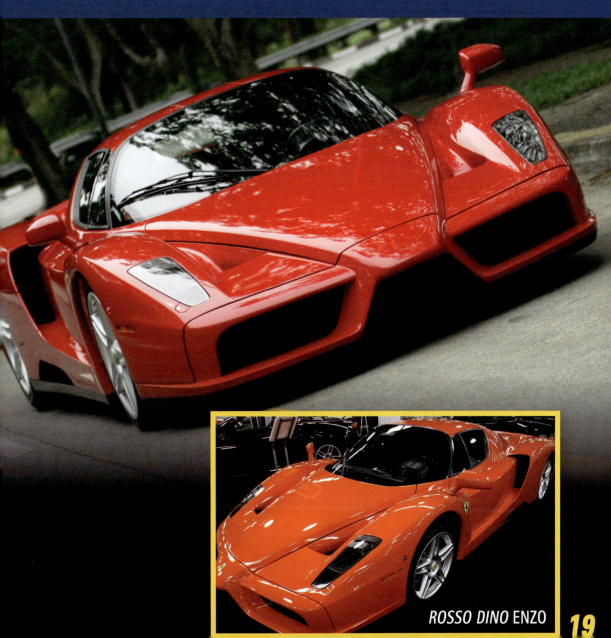

ROSSO DINO ENZO

THE CALIFORNIA
2008–2017

The Ferrari California debuted at the 2008 Paris Motor Show. It was a two-door, two-seat grand touring car, which is a luxury car that can reach high speeds and be driven long distances, inspired by the Ferrari 250 California. The 250 California was released in 1957 and was one of the most popular early Ferrari models. The modern Ferrari California only came as a convertible with **retractable** hardtop. It was the first Ferrari model to have that type of roof.

The California was the first front-engined Ferrari with a V-8. It was slightly less powerful than other Ferraris, with only 450 horsepower and a top speed of 193 miles (310.6 km) per hour. However, it could go from 0 to 60 miles (96.6 km) per hour in just 3.8 seconds.

> THE FIRST FERRARI CALIFORNIA WAS PRODUCED FROM 2008 TO 2014. IT WAS THEN UPDATED TO BECOME THE CALIFORNIA T, PICTURED HERE, WHICH WAS PRODUCED FROM 2014 TO 2017.

1962 FERRARI 250 GT CALIFORNIA SPYDER

THE 458 ITALIA
2009–2015

The Ferrari 458 Italia was designed to be the company's sportiest model in the V-8 lineup. It debuted at the 2009 Frankfurt Motor Show. Pininfarina and Ferrari Centro Stile designed the 458 Italia to be a compact, or space-saving, and aerodynamic car for Ferrari's V-8 class.

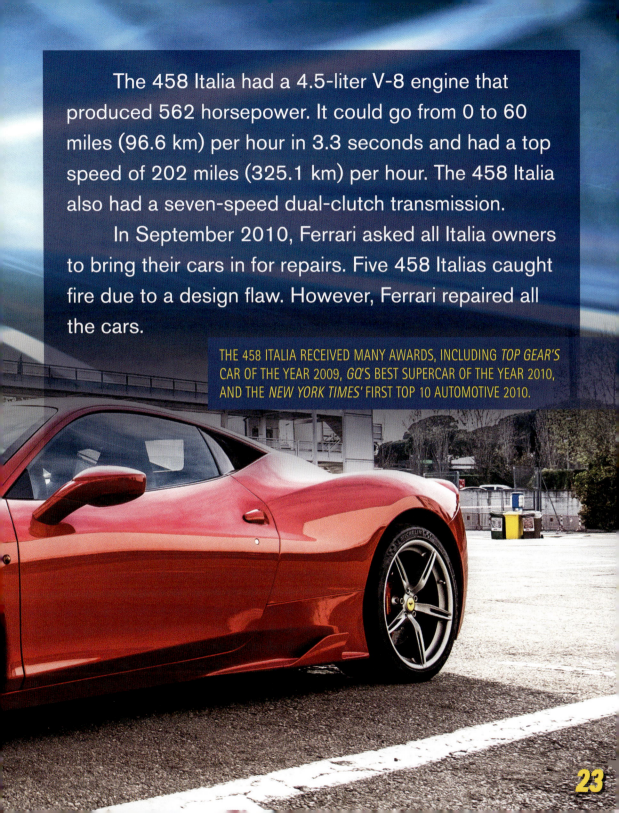

The 458 Italia had a 4.5-liter V-8 engine that produced 562 horsepower. It could go from 0 to 60 miles (96.6 km) per hour in 3.3 seconds and had a top speed of 202 miles (325.1 km) per hour. The 458 Italia also had a seven-speed dual-clutch transmission.

In September 2010, Ferrari asked all Italia owners to bring their cars in for repairs. Five 458 Italias caught fire due to a design flaw. However, Ferrari repaired all the cars.

THE 458 ITALIA RECEIVED MANY AWARDS, INCLUDING *TOP GEAR'S* CAR OF THE YEAR 2009, *GQ'S* BEST SUPERCAR OF THE YEAR 2010, AND THE *NEW YORK TIMES'* FIRST TOP 10 AUTOMOTIVE 2010.

THE FF
2011–2016

When Ferrari launched the FF, which stands for Ferrari Four, at the 2011 Geneva Motor Show, it was the most **versatile** car the company had ever created. The FF had four seats and was the first Ferrari to have four-wheel drive. The FF's **patented** four-wheel drive system, called 4RM, was different from those from other manufacturers. This system was 50 percent lighter than a normal four-wheel drive system.

> THE FF REPLACED THE 612 SCAGLIETTI, WHICH WAS PRODUCED FROM 2004 TO 2011. WHEN IT WAS LAUNCHED, THE FF COST $300,000 AND WAS SAID TO BE THE FASTEST FOUR-SEAT CAR IN THE WORLD.

612 SCAGLIETTI

      The FF could go from 0 to 62 miles (0 to 99.8 km) per hour in just 3.7 seconds and had a top speed of 208 miles (334.8 km) per hour. It had a 651-horsepower V-12 engine. Unlike many Ferraris, the FF had a lot of space for passengers and had a large trunk with plenty of room for luggage or other items, such as a stroller or a golf bag.

THE SF71H

As of 2018, Scuderia Ferrari drives the SF71H for F1 racing. It's the 64th single-seater car designed and produced by Ferrari to compete in the Formula One World Championships. This car is more aerodynamic and has wider tires than the previous single-seater, the SF70H. These changes are meant to make the car perform better on the track. Altogether, with fuel, water, and the driver, the SF71H only weighs about 1,616 pounds (733 kg).

New to the 2018 racing season, the SF71H features a structure to protect the cockpit, which is where the driver sits. Scuderia Ferrari's main drivers of the SF71H are Kimi Räikkönen, from Finland, and Sebastian Vettel, from Germany. Antonio Giovinazzi, from Italy, is the team's third driver. The SF71H made its debut on February 25, 2018, at Barcelona's Catalunya circuit.

IN PREVIOUS YEARS, SCUDERIA FERRARI'S CARS HAVE BEEN PAINTED DIFFERENT COLORS. HOWEVER, IN 2018, THE SF71H RETURNED TO AN ALL-RED PAINT JOB.

70 YEARS AND *BEYOND*

In September 2017, Ferrari held a two-day celebration at the Fiorano circuit for its 70th anniversary. During these two days, 120 historic cars competed for the title of Best of Show in two categories: Racing Car and Road Car. A 1953 340 MM Spider Vignale won Best of Show in the Racing Car category and a 1986 Testarossa Spider won Best of Show in the Road Car category. There was also an **auction** of 38 cars. These cars sold for a total of €63 million (about $74 million).

Ferrari continues to be one of the most popular sports car makers in the world. In the first three months of 2018, Ferrari had already sold 2,128 cars, 569 of them in the Americas. By the end of 2018, Ferrari expects to have sold more than 9,000 cars.

ON JUNE 5, 2018, FERRARI'S TURBO-CHARGED 3.9-LITER V-8 ENGINE WAS VOTED THE BEST ENGINE IN THE WORLD FOR THE THIRD YEAR IN A ROW AT THE 2018 INTERNATIONAL ENGINE OF THE YEAR AWARDS.

TIMELINE

February 18, 1898 ▸ Enzo Anselmo Ferrari is born in Modena, Italy.

1920 ▸ Ferrari begins driving for Alfa Romeo.

1939 ▸ Ferrari establishes Auto Avio Costruzioni.

1940 ▸ Auto Avio Costruzioni produces the 815.

1943 ▸ Ferrari moves Auto Avio Costruzioni to Maranello, Italy.

1947 ▸ The Ferrari 125 S debuts at the Piacenza circuit.

1948 ▸ Ferrari releases the 166 S, the 166 Inter, and the 166 MM.

1949 ▸ Ferrari wins its first 24 Hours of Le Mans.

1950 ▸ Scuderia Ferrari makes its Formula One debut.

1984 ▸ The Testarossa debuts.

2002 ▸ The Enzo Ferrari debuts.

2008 ▸ The California debuts.

2009 ▸ The 458 Italia debuts.

2011 ▸ The FF debuts.

2017 ▸ Ferrari celebrates its 70th anniversary.

2018 ▸ Scuderia Ferrari begins racing the SF71H.

GLOSSARY

aerodynamic: The qualities of an object that affect how easily it's able to move through the air.

auction: A public sale at which things are sold to those who offer to pay the most.

cylinder: A tube-shaped part of an engine.

design: The way something has been made. Also, to create the plan for something.

endurance: The quality of continuing for a long time.

exclusive: Available to only a few people, often because of high cost.

legacy: The lasting effect of a person or thing.

passenger: Someone riding on or in a vehicle.

patent: Rights given to a person by the government to make, use, or sell an invention. Or, to obtain those rights.

prototype: A first or early example that is used as a model for what comes later.

retractable: Able to be drawn or pulled back into something larger that usually covers it.

symbol: Something that stands for something else.

transmission: The part of a car or another vehicle that uses the engine's power to turn the wheels.

tsunami: A series of ocean waves caused by disruptions in the ocean.

versatile: Able to adapt, or change, to many different functions and activities.

INDEX

A
Alfa Romeo, 6, 9, 30
Auto Avio Costruzioni, 6, 30

C
California (car), 20, 21, 30
Corse Clienti, 12, 13

E
812 Superfast, 4, 5, 11
815, 6, 30
Enzo Ferrari (car), 18, 19, 30

F
Ferrari, Enzo, 4, 6, 7, 9, 18, 30
Ferrari Challenge, 12, 13
Ferrari 125 S, 4, 6, 7, 12, 30
Ferrari 166, 8, 30
Ferrari Four (FF), 24, 25, 30
Formula One, 10, 12, 14, 26, 30
458 Italia, 12, 22, 30

G
Giovinazzi, Antonio, 26
Grand Touring (GT) racing, 12

L
LaFerrari Aperta, 10, 11

P
Pininfarina, 17, 22
Portofino, 4, 5

R
Räikkönen, Kimi, 26

S
Scaglietti, 24, 25
Schumacher, Michael, 14
Scuderia Ferrari, 12, 14, 15, 26, 30
SF71H, 26, 30
Sivocci, Ugo, 6
Sportscar World Championship, 12

T
Targa Florio, 6
Testarossa, 16, 17, 28, 30

V
Vettel, Sebastian, 26

WEBSITES

Due to the changing nature of Internet links, PowerKids Press has developed an online list of websites related to the subject of this book. This site is updated regularly. Please use this link to access the list: www.powerkidslinks.com/hood/ferraris